Because of all the homeless animals in the world,
this book is dedicated to
those compassionate people
who adopt, foster and volunteer at animal shelters.

WILLIE WILSON'S WONDROUS TAILS ™

Written and Illustrated by Susan Castriota

Cover and Book Design: Faye Klein

First Edition 2012

www.wilsongetsadopted.com

Hi! My name is Wilson. Some call me Willie for short. My friends like to call me Willie Wilson!

My friends and I know a lot about bullies. Bullies come in many colors, shapes and sizes. You may know one or two yourself. Bullies are people (and dogs) who are mean. They are mean because they don't like themselves. They hurt others because they think it will make them feel powerful. But, that is not what makes someone powerful and important.

A bully may call you names or spread gossip about you. Marco, the Mean Mastiff, calls me a "Prissy Poodle in a Purse". He tells others that I was sick and abandoned because no one loved me. I know that is not true. But it still hurts me.

MEAN

Real dogs have purses

I feel sorry for Mean Marco. He is acting this way because he does not feel loved. I once felt this way until I was adopted and loved by my new family. I turn my hurt into pride and tell everyone about my new life. I can choose to ignore Marco's bad behavior because I know that those who really know me love me.

Wilson Won't Be Bullied
And Neither Will You!

A bully might be jealous of what you have. Spike likes her new, cool sunglasses and feels good wearing them. Debi, the Envious Doberman, tells everyone that Spike looks silly with her new shades. Envious Debi tries to knock Spike's glasses from her head. Spike feels very hurt.

Envy turns Debi into a bully. I tell Spike to ignore Envious Debi and to wear her sunglasses with confidence. Don't be ashamed of what you have or who you are. You are special! Some people might make fun of you because you have something they wish they had.

Spike Won't Be Bullied And Neither Will You!

Betty likes my sunglasses

Bullies might feel insecure when you can do things that they can't do. Sydney is a fast runner. Rascal, the Resentful Terrier, and his friends try to trip Sydney while he is running. They all laugh at Sydney. Rascal thinks if he bullies Sydney, the others won't notice that Sydney runs faster than he does.

Pedal faster, Cody!

I think you should reach out to those like Resentful Rascal and offer to run with them. Sydney can do that because he has the confidence that Rascal lacks. He understands that Rascal doesn't feel good about himself. Never let a Rascal slow you down!

Sydney Won't Be Bullied
And Neither Will You!

Come on Rascal, run with Nino and me.

A bully might make fun of the disabled or sick. Oliver has a health problem. He cannot run and play like the others. But Oliver is smart and clever in so many other ways. Ryder, the Rude Rottweiler, laughs and pokes fun at Oliver. Rude Ryder feels important by hurting defenseless Oliver.

Come on Bonnie
and Finnegan, let's go swimming.

Rude Ryder is not as important as he thinks he is. Lack of compassion turned Ryder into a bully. He cannot accept those who are different. One has to be stronger, kinder and believe in himself or herself to accept those who are different. I told Oliver that those with special needs can be accepted and have friends like everyone else.

Oliver Won't Be Bullied
And Neither Will You!

Oliver! Gizmo! Winston! I'm coming in.

Bullies may hide behind social media or computer screens. They are called cyber-bullies. Sushi and Violet are victims of cyber bullying. Bruno, the Bully Bulldog, made threats and spread untrue posts online about Sushi and Violet. Bully Bruno is using social media to hide his name and face.

I tell Sushi and Violet that Bruno is a coward. Immediately tell an adult about any cyber-bullying. Be careful when online. Ask your parents to block those like Bully Bruno. Speak up for yourself and others who are victims of cyber-bullying.

Sushi and Violet Won't Be Bullied And Neither Will You!

I hope you are never a victim or one who is a bully. If you see someone being bullied, be a friend and offer support. Seek help from a teacher, guidance counselor or parent.

Learn to laugh at yourself — use humor as your shield.

Bullying hurts inside and out. Be stronger than the bully.

A bully does not like himself and wants you to feel badly about yourself. You have control over how you feel. Bullies can hurt your feelings only if you let them! And remember…

Wilson Won't Be Bullied
And Neither Will You!

Sweet Dreams